BOBBIE COELHO was born near in Hampshire with her husband has always enjoyed poetry, but after being diagnosed with Parkinson's disease in 2002, she was particularly compelled to write as a way of putting things into perspective. Bobbie is a great fan of Forces Poetry (flowforall.org), and has had work published in two of their anthologies, *Voices of the Poppies* and *Poems of the Poppies*.

"My wish is that when people read this book, it will make them think a little more and reflect on their journey."
Bobbie Coelho, Autumn 2010

Finding the Light
Bobbie Coelho

For Steve Coelho
who has been my partner on the journey for 24 years.

I wish to thank
my sister in law, Anna Eades as well as Janet Bartlett,
who helped me enormously.

Finding the Light by Bobbie Coelho

Published in paperback in 2011 by Bobbie Coelho using SilverWood Books Empowered Publishing™

www.silverwoodbooks.co.uk

Copyright © Bobbie Coelho 2011

The right of Bobbie Coelho to be identified as the author of this work

has been asserted by her in accordance with the Copyright,

Designs and Patents Act 1988.

All rights reserved. No part of this publication may be reproduced,

stored in a retrieval system, or transmitted in any form or by any means,

electronic, mechanical, photocopying, recording or otherwise,

without prior permission of the copyright holder.

ISBN 978-1-906236-47-2

British Library Cataloguing in Publication Data

A CIP catalogue record for this book is available from the British Library

Set in Jenson Light by SilverWood Books

Printed in England on paper from sustainable sources

Finding the Light

You are born in the dark of the morning
And you think it's your destiny light
As you age, you realise it's a false one
Artificial, easily switched out

In older age, the day breaks
And you blink at the glint of the morn
The pieces of your life fit together
That is the day you are born

For Mothers Everywhere

Suddenly it's upon me
Today is Mother's Day
A woman, so brave
Worrying what the future
Will bring for her child to be

All the hardships that arise
Every single stage
(especially a teenager
—what a difficult age!)
And I wonder too,
As each stage passes by
Do you see yourself mirrored
In your child's life?

This love, so unusual
The greatest love of all
However, you turn out
Your mother is there through it all
Never saying, "I told you so",
"Why did you do that?"
She always has the strength to
Carry you through

When you're in trouble
However far away
Their love surrounds you
Every single day.

Morning Glory

I love my morning glory
It reaches to the sky
Then tumbles down again
Going all over the place
Just like a nosy gossip.

My morning glory is a blowsy tart
She's very forward
Winding her tendrils tenderly around
Caressing plants in her way
Choking them if she can

But in the morning such abundant colour!
Big cups of clear blue
Together with her crimson sister,
A joy to behold
Brightening up the dullest day

The flowers, though beautiful, are fleeting
Like our own lives they are soon gone
So we rejoice in our morning glory
Remembering to enjoy each flower, each day
And like the flower enjoy the sunshine while we can.

The Essence of Me

When I stand before this floor
I feel the ground opening up like never before
Tongue tied and unable to speak
Walking awkwardly on my feet

I was born a dragon child,
With fire in my heart which lights up my eyes
I can see you look surprised!
What power I have to fill you with zeal
Bring out the best that you always conceal
If I've said this once, I'll say it again
I am not the leader of men
I'm the one with a pen
Suggesting ways to perfect your plan
I'm not the sun dispensing warm rays
I am the moon who lightens dark ways
I am the voice in the still of the night
Reassuring that all will be right
When your confidence has got up and gone
I am the one who tell you you're strong

My spirit could last evermore
But my body is not playing – you know the score
Many a person has written me off
But no one can make me stop

Most people say that dragons aren't real
But in China their power has great appeal

But, thinking again, that's probably true
For I'm invisible to all but you.

The Woman in the Picture*

The picture came from the past
Washed with disturbing emotion
From the largest tidal wave
Changing the world forever
As if the very film
Which captured the image
Was laced with the sorrow she felt

What happened to that woman?
Does anybody know?
The world saw it happening
Stood by and did nothing

The world is so tiny, really
There's no such thing as
"A land far away of which we
know nothing"
She's my sister and my mother
My father and my brother
Affecting us all, good or bad
We must stick together

The woman in the picture
Has haunted me for years

When I look at her face
I am always reminded
What a broken heart looks like
How potently I see it

And how passionately
it speaks to me.

*This picture is a famous one from WW2, showing the invasion of the Sudetenland, and shows a woman saluting with one hand and a handkerchief in other, crying.

It's Christmas – Again!

It's Christmas Day and the dinner
Is gently steaming away
I'm trying to shut out the din
Coming from the lounge all day
The family fight is building nicely–
With fists flying every way
They've been at the spirits again!
Making them shirty and angry
The only spirit they're sharing
Is fighting with knuckles bared

And then there's Grandma whining
About the old days when during the war
Her family said she could do better
Than good for nothing Granddad
Oh God – how long can I last?

Am I safe penned in the kitchen?
Swigging from the neck of Gordon's Dry Gin
Trying to forget my shattered nerves
Can I forget the state they've put me in?

There are times when I hate my family
And I just want to pack up and go
But if I do I'll know they'll find me
When they want some freshly washed clothes.

Premature

He had such a tiny body
And a desperate desire for life
His whole body heaved
As he gasped for breath
Born before his time.

How I longed to stroke
His doll-like body
To run my hand down his back
And tell him I loved him
In my mind I begged: let him live.

The Last Roses of Summer

The last roses of summer softly brush my cheek
They are scarce now, missing summer heat
The roses are pure white, but have no scent
They are a reminder of a summer heaven-sent.

Against my skin, the roses feel soft and smooth
Large petals touch me like silk as I move
It feels sad that these flowers will soon be gone
Wishing that next summer would quickly come along.

When the rose bush is in full bloom, it is like a snowdrift in summer
A cascade of white flowers, taking your eyes to them like a lover
Of course the rose has very sharp thorns
It reminds me so much of life, when you take it by the horns
Pain and pleasure often come closely together.

As a reminder of the long summer days
I shall pick a perfect rose and preserve it for always
It's the only way to bear winter's rage
By looking at the summer rose in the appropriate page.

When winter has gone, Spring will come
Along with the first flowers, and hopefully, the sun
The rose bush will awake from sleep
I wonder if next summer will be so sweet?

Age to Youth

I know that you are still in your youth
But I feel you should face the truth
life is as short as a passing dream
Things aren't straightforward as they seem
So let me tell you what you should know
Each day you should aim for the stars
Be proud of what you are.

Tell your children you love them lots
Eagerly encourage the talent they've got
Raise them to know what's right
They are the future, so make it bright
Guide them along life's rocky highway
They will also teach you much some day.

You see me now as tired and old
Sometimes now, I feel the winter cold
I was young not so long ago
Free to choose my life, I was told
Look deep into my eyes
Time is not on your side
For once, I remember, there was a day
And it wasn't that far away
When the future used to be me.

Lost Chance

I dreamt I saw my daughter in a dress of creamy white
Her eyes just like diamonds, sparkling in the night
And held her arms out to me for a future she could see
But I shook my head, for it didn't look so bright to me
I caught the look in her eyes as I slowly turned away
It will haunt me until my dying day.

Striking Gold

Most people spend their lives digging for a seam of gold
The hole is very deep and empty when they get grey and old
They won't find what their looking for digging in the ground
The treasure they seek is scattered all around

The sheer joy of living and seeing the beauty of another day
To laugh, or even to redeem yourself for a remark you've made
Being fortunate to call another person friend
Remembering the ones beloved, but never seen again

These are the things I call striking gold
But some people keep on digging and will never be told.

The Circle of Life

The circle of life is always there
A new life born, bringing joy beyond compare
A person dies, the sadness of family is forever there
A life whose journey is complete, all lessons learned
A new person who has respect to earn
The circle of life is never finished
It grinds on and on into eternity bringing changes to me and you.

Lost

Did the earth move for you Darling?
It did for me
The earth fell from beneath my feet
The night I was betrayed
Like that man in the garden years ago

You always told me you loved me
I left my home and family to be by your side
Our blood was one
Our bond so strong
Now, all gone

The world is full of couples
Yet sometimes I feel quite alone
Roughly cut off from my past
And very fearful for the future
How will I face the world now?

I wish I knew what went wrong
So many years to throw away
For nothing, except fear
But getting someone younger
Will not save you from old age

But, the time is coming for you to beware
Each day my confidence grows, I become stronger
And I will fight with all my heart
To make sure our children don't suffer
Whatever you do.

Found

Your confidence gives pleasure to all your friends around
You have come on in great leaps and bounds
What was lost, is now most definitely found
I can hardly believe that's come about
It's barely a year since your life was turned inside out.

From those lonely first faltering steps
Contentment you never thought you'd get
Working for promotion was not easy, I bet
Now you are on the sure-fire ladder of success.
The next few years will be the best ever yet.

Strength and bravery inside the great unknown
Can you see how much you've grown?
Now you'll never settle for second best
A few sad memories, but then life has a new zest
Remember, you're a cut above the rest.

True Fear

In youth you are confident and so very sure
Health and vitality ooze from every pore
When you get older and wrinkles appear in every place
One horrible thought smacks you in the face
What if there's nothing beneath that charming carapace?

Parting

Goodbye is such a little word
Not difficult to pronounce
Not difficult to spell
Oh, but, so difficult to say

The word sometimes sticks in your throat
Through your tears
All the things you meant to say
Left unsaid

Goodbye is a word-bomb
Devastating your life
Feeling desolation, something ending
I much prefer hello.

Out with the Old

Spring-cleaning is such fun!
Even happier when the task is done
Carefully clearing out each drawer with care
You'll be surprised what you find there!
Things you lost years ago
Hey presto! Suddenly appear before your eyes

Why did I keep such tat?
Am I as sentimental as that?
I certainly have lived without them
But, some things you throw away
Are desperately needed once upon a day
To help you live your life your way.

Of course, some things you don't toss out
Most intimate and precious things without a doubt
Like love letters confirming the love you have earned
They will never be burned
Or put in a plastic sack
Consigned into the rubbish bin at the back.

One Little Bird

Our little Henry is such a lovely bird
He's full of life, so very chirpy
And so very happy
Even though he's dying
I held his coffin today
It made me so sad
To hear his joyful song
Regretfully, not for very long

He'll soon be a distant memory
I hope God will care for him
When he goes on his way
All on his own
Where we cannot follow

Life's not fair, is it?
To take our lovely yellow bird
I'm dreading that final morning
Going downstairs
Finding him on the floor
Quite dead.

Our Last Supper

The Christmas party is here at long last
Workmates discussing stories from the past
Others revealing holiday plans
Some travelling to foreign lands
Seeing old faces returning makes me glad
But the occasion is also quite sad
It is our last supper as one team
Nothing lasts forever, it seems

I've been told there'll be a joint party next year
But it won't have the same easy cheer
The cracks from the split will be clearly seen
We'll move across the road very soon
But might as well move to the moon.

Remember This

Now the 11th day of November is here
It doesn't bring very much cheer
The weather is dank and bitterly cold
In mourning for brave men of old.

The war started one day in late July
When Princip decided an Archduke would die
And made two common nations, united by blood
Grind themselves down in the mire and the mud.

Lots of men rushed to sign on
Poor innocents: didn't know what would come
They would suffer pain and know such fear
In a dark, stinking hole most of them died
Nobody ever stopped to ask: why?

They must have been afraid
I wonder, did they pray?
Or did they just feel betrayed
By God and their country on certain days.

The list of names on the Menin Gate
A body with no grave: a terrible fate
A whole generation, just swept away
 No one will know how many died in a day
At Ypres, the Somme and Passchendale.

Many loved ones were left weeping
Mothers, fathers, sisters and wives
Had lost precious lives
Memories were all they were keeping
Now that their loved ones lie silently sleeping.

However, one fact I seem to recall
The seeds of the Second, lie in the Great War
Old men watched their children die, like before,
So nothing was changed, nothing at all.

Swan Flotilla

There's a park behind our house
As beautiful as nature can be
It is very peaceful: a sight you really ought to see
With grass so lush and trees every shade of green
Lots of wildlife lurking in the bushes
And ducks rustling in the rushes
Trying to gobble the food before it reaches the others

There is one sight, which eclipses all the others
You'll see (if you're very lucky)
 A close-knit family of swans gliding on the water
 Father, mother, sister and one little brother
Staying close together, looking out for one another
We named them the flotilla

Their pure white wings looked like sails as they paddled
On the lake and down the crystal river
With father proudly swimming at the fore
Little brother as the stern, his tail moving like a tiller
They looked for the world like a ghostly, silent flotilla.

If you stood to admire their lovely, graceful, stance
They would head towards you, hoping just by chance
To see some food appearing, whilst giving an admiring glance
The family would anchor themselves by the river bank
Four swans sitting silently, watching you without blinking
I often wondered what they were really thinking

Song for a Little Girl

Abandoned, unloved and alone
No family to call her own
Lying in a plastic hospital cot
The only thing she's got

That tiny little girl
Is now out in the world
I hope someone cared
And took her in as theirs.

Windows

Do you spend your life looking through windows?
Or are you on the inside?
If so, do you stare at the ones freezing outside?
They are strangers to you
Part of them wants to run and hide
But the other half wants some warmth too
If they only had the courage and tried

Do you really want them?
Maybe they're not your style
Perhaps you think those strangers
Are really not worthwhile?
Why don't you try and usher them inside?
If you don't reach out to them
They'll freeze and slowly die.

Old Men on Remembrance Day

What stories could those old men tell?
Of war and pain, running into hell?
I see those faces pinched and drawn
Parading down Whitehall on a November morn.

The silence is announced by a bugler's blast
The crowd stands still and quiet at last
The old men have their own secret thoughts
Of comrades fallen and battles fought.

They probably wondered how they survived
When so many of their friends died.
The living grow old and grey
Unlike their comrades who faded away.

So when that cold, November day is approaching
Remember those old men soldiers who did the fighting
The ones who died and who survived for our cause
They gave their yesterdays and paid the highest price of all.

My Lost Baby

I was young and very, very green
Not knowing what could have been
The two of us, swore undying love
As we both gazed at the stars above
Reality came on that fateful day
The price that only I would pay.

My pregnancy couldn't be concealed
My lover took to his heels
At seventeen I was alone and in disgrace
Not daring even to show my face
In a cold institution my baby was born
On a lovely summer's morn.

I was frightened when my labour pains came
No one there to ease my pain
She was so lovely, I named her Mary Jane,
When she was put in my arms I felt such love
My emotions were on a cloud above.

I knew one day we had to part
It very nearly broke my heart
A couple took her away to a loving home
I gave her up and left alone
I wish I could have seen her grow.

Inside a painful cry echoes down the years
My thoughts of her bring me to tears
I wonder if she looks like me.

My life's dream would be to see
The beautiful woman she had grown to be
I would love to find my girl
Nothing would part us, not in this world.

New Year

How I love the midnight chime
And singing Old Lang Syne
I feel my chin quiver at this time
In Remembrance of people most dear
Who are not with us here
Family, acquaintances and friends
A list that would never end

The hour is upon us at last
And the old year has now passed
It is part of history now
Even if the problems still hang around
Maybe a solution can be now found

Before the New Year begins
I go over the changes I'll bring
It will be a brand new start
I promise that from the heart
To get fit and live a healthy life
To treasure my friends most dear

Two happy Rabbits, we'll paint our hutch
Give it our loving touch
Improve rooms and make them easy to clean
Get rid of what we don't need
Prepare the garden for its best show yet
We want the biggest riot of colour we can get

I'll always love the New Year
The year starts with my goals set very clear
A new start brings comfort after strive
But if last year brought much joy and pleasure
You can treasure the memory forever

Something occurs to me
Each day is a new beginning
So perhaps I should change my thinking
Make a resolution each day
To make the most of life while I may.

Here I Build My Church

Here I stand in this place
Towering above the human race
A silent witness to all your emotions
Whether believer or not, I get the notion
You want to thank God for my conception
There's a man who loves without exception.

When paying me a visit, most people are astounded
They feel a miracle was created the day I was founded
That God could give a man such vision
To build a church with such precision
Gaudi gave his whole life, unsparing
Before I was finished, he was dying.

Although abandoned for many years by Man
The Grand Architect, who knows all our plans
Will make sure my work is completed
The visionary who designed my being
Is lying, deep in my womb, for safekeeping
He is now honoured, as well he should be
For giving Barcelona a monument to God's See.

Whether very old or very modern
The church is of God's holy pattern
Christianity is very old
It has never made man's heart grow cold
Whatever the year, whether old or new
There is only one Truth, handed down from ages anew.

Swimming

Come in, they said
The water is lovely
So I jumped in
They are right
The water is warm and soothing
I'm swimming along, enjoying the feeling
I am free and happy
So glad I'm alive

They didn't tell me though
In warm water, sharks suddenly appear
So keep a sharp lookout
But if you leave warm water and go into cold
You freeze all alone.

Dance

All our life we dance to the music of life
To find happiness is all we need to survive
The style and pace of the rhythm is ever changing
 As we dance to the music of life

Music reflects our feelings as we rush from day to day
Never really seeing how time is floating away
Our moves reflect where we are through all those little stages
Showing our way through each decade of aging

There comes a time when the music becomes much slower
Most of the dancing is virtually over
Eventually, looking back feeling deeply contented
For now it's all in your head, memories never relenting.

Choices

As you grow and roll along
Thinking life is a long, happy song
And your body will never go wrong
Always believing you'll be young and strong
One day you suddenly stiffen
Your body refuses to listen
Then you're sitting in a consulting room
Filled with fear and gathering gloom
Waiting to hear your fate
Have you left it all too late?
Then your life as you know it shatters
But you find out what really matters
It's not fame or fortune – nothing like!
But silently beg for your life.

A Squash Game

Two men walk out on a squash court
Ready to play a game, hard-fought
The spectators are looking intense
Anticipating a good event
There is a definite gladiatorial air
With much shouting at the duelling pair

A toss of the racquet decides
Who starts the game with a serve
The ball hits the wall and boomerangs back
Both players are on the attack
They hope their weaknesses won't show
As they psyche each other out
Determination on their faces says it all
They put each other through their paces
The referee watches like a hawk
Everything that happens on the court

The game is only for two
One will win and the other will lose
But there is still plenty of time
For the both to find a sign
To kill the other one's shots
Both silently pray
They will win the day.

Island Girl

Blast and damn!
I can't walk properly again.
My feet slowly gather speed
I look comical indeed!
Although people sometimes stare,
I have my pride
I always have to remind myself
I'm still me inside.

Yes, I'm still me inside
But on the outside things have changed:
My feet sometimes freeze and I can't move
I sometimes dribble and move really slowly
Which makes me feel very lowly
I feel I still have a lot to prove
My mind is sound, but my body that lets me down.

My memory is far too good
I remember far more than I should
I remembered once what I had lost
I cried, then realised how much this disease has cost
Sometimes I feel I'm stranded on a desert island
With only a line attached to a healthy majority
Mostly, I know how lucky I am:
it could have been much worse
I have cried many times, but I won't die
I am loved: it is enough.

The Wedding

It's a lovely day for a wedding
Overlooking the Isle of Skye
There's a touch of magic in this place
Just like the look of happiness on a friend's face.
We all gathered together, strangers and friends
To wish them joy which never ends
The ceremony was simple but tugged the heart
Then the couple walk out together to a new start.

White Flowers

Little children lying dead
Like white flowers stained deepest red
Heaven knows what went through their heads
While their parents watched with dread
Listening for every tread

Now little girls can't use their charms
Nor walk down the aisle on their father's arm
And what about the little boys?
They will no longer need their toys

With every bullet and every bomb
Their parents dreams are dead and gone
How will they ever carry on.

Emily

Emily is such a beautiful black cat
Although very laid back, she knows where it's at
Putting all the neighbourhood dogs in a rage
She sashays up to them, clearly unafraid
The barking dogs are puzzled and left in a daze.

Emily loves the children who live all around
And they love her too, whether lost or not
Emily is always 'found'
She has a talent for getting locked in
Does she create a din!

Emily's so lovely and a daddy's girl
She seemed to love him most in all the world
But lately: well, the little pickle!
Emily has become quite fickle.

Life's Journey

Isn't it funny how clocks rule us
Relentlessly tick-tocking
Letting us know they are never far away
We are their slaves
Sometimes lucky ones escape.

Our lives are like vibrant exciting dreams
Sometimes short, sometimes dramatic
When starting on this journey
Decisions we take sometimes touch us forever.
Yet you have to decide which way to go.

Some roads are straight and secure,
Very flat and colourless
The others more rocky and hilly
Yet pure joy is felt – and deep sorrow!
One road leads to death in life, the other is life.

Anthem for Janet

The sun is shining bright
Open your eyes to a bright new light
For this is a brand new day
Look in the mirror and say
Today my life starts anew
I'll move on to pastures new
There's a big world out there
With people who really care

Begone all trouble and strife
Today is the first day of a brand new life.

Hope

When you feel tired and want to give up
All you see is tinted with grey
Just remember the winter's chill
Always makes you feel weary and ill.

After winter comes Spring
When the life source bubbles within
As the bushes around turn green
New hope surges within us again.

After the Spring comes the sun!
The lazy days will soon come
Enjoying the lovely English air
How could anyone have a care?

Life is so short, just remember
In deepest January, a thought to ponder
You'll soon see the swallow
A smell those lovely summer flowers.

A Mantra for Living

Some people are always looking through windows
Their lives are spent living in shadows
A few pluck up courage and actually start believing
A few tottering steps into the sunlight leave them blinking
And then they are talking and breathing and giving
Then they know what it means to be living.

People

Sometimes it's hard to see the good in life
When you turn on your TV, seeing war and strife
It can easily make someone feel that human beings stink
Please take a minute to consider this and think.

Instead of looking and seeing the worst
Flip the coin and look at the good first
For most people really are good you know
Surprising when the hard knocks begin their cruel blows.

Just look at the appeals on TV
Or the listen to the radio
The charity appeals for donations
You'll see money mounting up
Consciences stirring throughout the nation
So, when you smile at people
They feel happy too
They'll be more likely to smile at you too.

Freak

Tell me how long does it take
To realise you're a freak?
To be pointed at in the street
The people, whispering close by
"Is she OK?" Oh, how I wanted to cry!

Horrified, you realise they mean you
You were never the sort to turn heads
Well, now you do
You want to hide
Losing your pride.

Feeling sad all the way home
I wish I hadn't come
I know they mean no harm
I must develop a tougher skin
To prevent people looking in.

Workmates

Today the sun shined on us
As we sat in the warm sunshine
We relaxed in the pub garden
Our whole section gathered there
At Hazel's leaving do

Hazel's going on promotion
She'll be sorely missed
Her cheerful smile and snappy dressing
You will never know when she cries
You only see her pleasure

Sitting closely to people you know
Yet are strangers
They display their smiling faces
Carefully concealing their thoughts
Behind freshly painted masks

What lies behind their smiling visages
In the night, when dreams and nightmares
Rule their minds and their souls stripped bare
No one will ever know
For in the morning, the mask is worn once more.

Football Commentators

Football is called the beautiful game
Its top players are widely acclaimed
And most of them are very skilled
So why is the game being killed
By people who dissect the match
They talk so much crap
Why don't they just shut up?
Sick as parrot indeed!
The team have come here to win
How can they say such silly things?
They could do with a shock
Something to wake their brains up
Or, failing that, gagging with a smelly sock!

A Lover's Waltz
(for Steve Coelho)

Give me a kiss in the morning
When we feel the sun's warming rays
It reminds me of our earliest days
The sun never stopped shining
Together, we made plenty of hay.

Give me a kiss at break time
It was always you from the start
Your smile captured my heart
The light of your love embraced me
So I bid farewell to the dark.

Give me a kiss at midday
You love highlights my way
For you will always come first
It was you who gave water
Preventing me from dying of thirst.

Give me a kiss in the evening
Before the night has begun
And there is no summer sun
When all my fears are spun
And hold me ever so tight
Until the dark takes flight.

A Special Journey

Three wise men followed a star
It guided them through lands afar
They travelled by day and night
Guided by that shining, bright light
The notion came in a dream
To visit a newborn King, who always reign supreme.

Then suddenly, the star's movement stopped
It rested over an inn's stable block
The men presented the baby with special things
Which foretold what the baby's life would bring
It was the best moment of their lives
One they would remember with pride.

Now, we are like those three men
At our birth, our star rises
And brings with it plenty of surprises!
We follow our star wherever it goes
But there is something I really want to know
When our star finally falters and descends
What will we find at our journey's end?

Time

Most people say time flies
It disappears before your eyes
Whenever I consider time
I compare my life
To a river quickly running by.

Like a torrent you enter the world
In a trice, the babe becomes a cheeky schoolgirl
Then a teenager, a woman and a wife
How quickly and silently goes our life!

Before you know it, you're old
I remember, when young, being told
When you reach Twenty-one, time flies
Now I know that person didn't lie
Like a river, my life has nearly run by.

Dreaming of Colours

Winter's chills are gone
Spring has already sprung
How I love the warming thought
That summer is knocking at the door!

The snowdrops have bloomed and died
The spring flowers are about to expire
Summer flowers are on their way
The bedding plants are on display.

I sit and dream of long, hot summer days
In the garden my imagination gets carried away
The hot pinks and oranges are all around
With colours so loud, you can almost hear their sound.

Hidden Hands

If you're so low and blue that you can barely eat
And feel that all your life is one long defeat
Your low cry will be heard
Hidden hands will pull you to your feet
They'll surround you with their loving
Making you feel very tall
Showing that your life is not a failure after all
Where this feeling comes from I do not know
But it lets you know you're not on your own
Maybe you think I'm mistaken but, believe me it is true
If those hands helped me, they'll certainly help you.

Looking

Look at the world with a child's eyes
I'll bet you will be surprised
At the deep green of the grass and bluest clearest sky
All the flowers have such lovely colours
While they juggle for attention with each other.
Everything you see is bright and new
Blinkers fall off and your sight is renewed.

Divided Souls

Somewhere I have a sister whose heart beats in similar time
Pumping round the blood which is exactly mine
Our mother didn't want us, so she gave us both away
I wonder did she ever live to regret that day?

Every time I walk around a new place
I am on the lookout for my sister's face
All I know is her Christian name
And that she is my identical twin, so we look the same.

I feel her presence surround me with a comforting squeeze
And her voice calling me through the summer breeze
We are twin souls torn apart from birth
Still walking around on this huge earth.

Sometimes I feel her emotions running through my head
Especially in the quiet of my lonely bed
My life is spent searching for my other skin
My identity, my other half – where are you
Where have you been?

Wash Day Greens

My husband's just washed my knickers
I can't believe what I've seen
What used to be pure white
Is now a dark shade of green!

Born from Fire

This island rose from the deepest depths
Released by a reluctant sea
With all guns blazing
The land pushed itself free
But now it is staid and very tame

But the sea has not forgotten
As the waves break; anger not assuaged
You can almost hear the whisper
"I want you back
You will come back
One day."

The Nightwatchman
or The Heron on the Lake

He visits the lake
At the close of day
Gliding confidently but low
Like a land-locked albatross

Suddenly he stops
Folding his huge wings
Peering like an old man
With the sharpest of eyes

We've seen him stand
Stock still for hours
Those gleaming, intelligent eyes
Just watch and wait…

Portrait of a Hero

The one who knows that
our skin tone may be different
and although our beliefs may not be the same
Underneath we are all the same family
Who doesn't see the stereotype
But recognises something in themselves
That the destination in life is the same
Wise enough to know the journey is not the same
For everyone
The one who works for the greater good
Who thinks of others, not just themselves
The one who carries on day by day
In the background, barely noticed
A good person in a crisis
Not judgemental, but understanding
Who wakes up every morning
Not bitter
Rather believing how lucky they are
Full of the pure joy of being alive
Whilst other poor nations struggle to survive.
Smiling as they walk
Infecting their neighbours with warmth going to work
To be humble enough realise that we have all
Created the society we live in
Although we may complain

That's what a hero is to me.

A Prayer

Make me happy not sad
For what I have, make me glad
Keep me sane, don't drive me mad
Help me do good, not bad.

Although now fully grown
Please let the child in me show
So wherever I go
My personality glows.

Memories

Hong Kong was like a breath of fresh air
(I bet that makes you laugh)
People running round
Looking like pilchards
Tinned in tomato sauce.

Macau was a lady
She'd seen better days
But on the day we met her
The pride of her faded glory
Shone through.

But, then one day we landed
In paradise
The land of smiles
Was warm and welcoming
We were happy.

Have you ever had that feeling?
Both exhilarating and sad
That you must treasure every moment
Knowing you'll never have it again?
We did.

Words on a Tombstone in Arnhem

"His life a beautiful memory
His death a silent grief."

Walking around a war cemetery one day
My eyes caught some words etched on a stone
Two lines, that's all they were: so full of grief!
Those words said so much – so beautiful beyond belief

A life cut down before his time
Harsh punishment, but he committed no crime
Now he lies here, long dead
Sleeping with a stone at his head.

As I walked I pondered on his life
What was he like, did he have a family and wife
Was he fearful, or elated as the battle
commenced, oh I hope he didn't know
He was outnumbered.
It was too hectic for that
No time for feelings before entering the fray
But like so many, caught in a trap and
The flower cut.

Those words, written years ago
In that Dutch cemetery are written in my soul
And the war still goes on
Forever, with no end
Only his family's dried bitter tears
Remember he is here.

So often I get tired looks
Why do I read history books?
A hand reaches back through the years
But the past affects us today.

Father and Daughter Reunion

Death took you just as the last rays
Of the summer sun were fading
I knew you wouldn't be lonely
But when you left
This world became too hollow
In my dark and deepest sorrow
I knew I had to follow

A year has passed and now
I set out to meet you
My darling daughter
The world was much too shallow
My heart was in dark shadow
So meet me as I travel on the road
Where no one can follow.

Sam

It's funny how the world turns without you even knowing
Not realising exactly how children are growing
It only seems like yesterday when Sam was a tiny baby
Screaming loudly frequently, nearly driving everyone crazy
Next week that little boy will be ten years old
Bursting with intelligence and becoming very bold
Trying on his new leather coat, I realise with surprise
Sam has grown into a fine young man before my eyes.

What Is a Soldier to Me?

When I see a person in olive green
In the street, or on a TV screen
It takes me back to knights of old
The feats of Agincourt years ago
And then to Wellington's brave band
Who drove Napoleon from Spanish lands
And thence on to both World Wars
Like lions they fought, not knowing what for
Giving their best – who can ask for more?

The person in green is the spirit of this land
When they reach out, feel the pulse in the hand
The brotherhood closer than any blood tie
They rely on each other to live and to die
Lionhearts of the country in which they serve
Cradling Albion, its freedom to preserve
It is because of them I can freely speak
Not fearing the rush of draconian feet.

We mark our loss with the poppy flower
Every November, but I still feel the power
Of the truest saying from Shakespeare's pen
A Band of Brothers – the greatest of Men.

The Twilight Zone

There is a well-kept secret
A place no one wants to go
It's called the Twilight Zone
You enter it alone
Nobody wants to know
When you're in the Twilight Zone

All you have to do
For people to be fearful of you
Is to mention in one breath
'Injury' and 'brain' their vivid
Imagination will do the rest.

Happiness

The happy laughter of children
Enjoying the bright sunny day
Is the most wonderful tonic you can wish for
To brush the clouds away
In addition, there is the garden
So colourful, like a parrot showing
Its plumage to the sun
What more can you ask
To chase the blues away?

The Telling

It is early in the morning
Another day is dawning
At the preying time
As the army wife lies
Fitfully sleeping
Suddenly she hears
A sound she dreads
And fears
At the family door
A flash of shock hits her
Like the bullet which
Killed her husband
A few short hours ago.

Now the company waits
Downstairs
To break the news
It's the telling time

Alone with her children
Not a family anymore.

Rudderless

The poppy still leaches its red every day
I often wonder will it ever go away.
This rudderless ship called England
Has run a deal off course
So we wait for fairer weather
Later on, come what may
England, my England,
Always stay.

Stratford on Avon

The place is very modern
With long roots going back far into the past
Narrow streets once plodded by Shakespeare
Resonate with echoes everlasting
The Bard knew people and realised
Human nature rarely changed
Driven by strong emotion
Irrationally behaved the same
Thus pushing self-destruction
Something we've forgotten
In this day and age.

Beached

The flowers in the garden
Have lost their scent for sure
The sun never shows its face here at all
People are changing, some are rotten to the core
Is this what it's like to be alive
But not living anymore?

Prawn Knickers

Do prawns have knickers?
I wonder if they do!
The question I would put is:
Would they be pink or would they blue?

I suppose when they are cold
The answer must be blue
The chillier the water
The darker the hue!

But of course they are nosy
Which leads to the cooking pot
The knickers change to pink
When the prawns get hot.

Rorke's Drift

And did those feet in Victorian times
March through that thick, brown sand so fine?
Red coats marching through the hot sun
In time?
And does the ring of those fine Welsh voices
Still ring?
In that uplifting way only the Welsh sing?
As battle raged and bullets pinged

Through fire and spear the Regiment stood
Did that song give them the extra strength they sought?
Through the years, does that song still sound
In Rorke's Drift and around?
As it did nearly two hundred years before?
And will it sound evermore?

Road to Nowhere

What happened to the English
The "mustn't grumble" generation?
Who used to walk tall and proud
Wearing a happy morning smile
Full of a reason and contentment
Tell me, where have they gone?

They have been replaced
By unhappy, unsmiling faces
Twisted with malice, envy and complaint
We have every creature comfort
How is it we are empty inside?

Has the world changed so much?
Just when did our nation tear itself apart?
What happened to the noble English heart?

Joe Bonamassa

Hey Joe!
Thanks for a brilliant show
You and your guitars
Are superstars!

Tell me though, which is true?
Did those guitars pluck your strings
Or do you make those guitars sing?
Whichever way it was last night
The journey was a pure delight.

First you made them sob with pain
Then lightening up once again
Those guitars bubbled with joy
Then you played my favourite song.
It wasn't to wash away the pain
Sloe Gin: slow, deep, so deep I sang along
My brain swimming in a higher plane.

So thank you for the music Joe
Long live the music and your guitars.

I Was Robbed

"I could," he said. "I probably could.
At least - I could if I tried."
I'll never know the heights I could fly
I could be like Father Christmas
Flying through the night sky
Or I could have been King of the World
If only I had tried.

The Drum

I am an army wife
Where my husband goes
I follow, however I can
Trudging the country's highways
Near and far from home
Even my heart beats to the drum
That always calls me home

Marrying a soldier brings a lot of joy
But also much hard work
As a mobile life will bring
He is proud to serve his country
His regiment, his King
Possessions we have not many
Except our girl and boy

Now he's posted far away
Standing on the dockside
Feeling dead and hollow
For the ballot paper I just held
Refused to let me follow
Children by my side I wave to him
How do I tell them, pray?
To look upon their father
For it may be the last time they may.

Miscarriage

Devastation has visited us
Dressed in scarlet tears
Every drop stirring our deepest fears
The baby whose birth was set
To brighten up our years,
Has silently left us now
Without a warning sound
The sadness is still with us
As the child turns sharply round
And makes the journey home.

A Soldier of the Queen
(for Peter)

I met a brave man yesterday
In Brighton on our D Day
His news shocked me to the core
About the cost of going to war

Not the money, but the important thing
Is the human cost: the result that war brings
In the Falkland campaign: so many took their lives!
How much they must have suffered inside

I know what suicide does to the lives
Of the parents, the children, the wives
"If only I'd listened" is the refrain
Constantly echoing around their brain

Oh my God the pain!
Such a deep, indelible, pain
Those memories play again
Again and again and again

I know what the feeling is like
To see a face filled dislike
Sometimes even scurry by
Afraid to even catch their eye

Do you know where that man has been?
He was a soldier of the Queen
God knows what he's seen
What he didn't bargain for

When he went to war
His life would change for evermore

The day he signed on
His families also signed along.

Lorna

I hear her voice, hardly speaking
My heart is rhythmically beating
I can barely see her face
Telling me she's been in my place

I feel she's giving me the score
Of what her life held in store
I've only seen pictures of her
But what a lovely mother-in-law.

An Ode to a Poppy

There is no colour so intense
No rose which lasts so long
As the poppy's dramatic look

No flower so fragile
Yet comes again every year
As the poppy fields at home

No other reminder is needed
Of the innocent blood long spilt
Except the blooming poppy's dripping red.

A Christmas Story
(Reprise)

It happened a long time ago
A story from wise men of old
To Mary, an angel appeared,
Saying "Don't be afraid, my dear",
You are special, the chosen one
To give birth to God's only son

What Joseph thought is quite hazy
Did he think Mary'd gone crazy?
With Mary he stayed through it all
Accepting whatever should befall
Mary was big with child
When the census call went nation wide
Ordered back to the town of Joseph's kin

They finally arrived at that tiny place
So it appeared did most of the human race
In Bethlehem; no shelter they found
Although they walked up and down the town
Just a lowly stable left to lay their tired heads

Bur, it was there that Mary gave birth
To the child who would bring redemption to the earth

What relevance, you ask?
Some fable dredged up from the past?
Well, forget the angels and things
Think about the message of hope this story brings

The meaning should be quite clear
For this miracle happens every day of the year
In a labour ward nearby
A new mother looks with wondering eyes
Into the face of her newborn child
At the future, and what the infant achieves
That's the miracle I feel.

Tracy's Wish

If wishes were granted
I'd travel the land
Scattering fairy dust
Fine as sand
As my left hand scattered
The dust I would say
Cure all ills and
Pain go away.

With my right?
Oh that fairy dust would
Be special indeed
I would ask that everybody
Got what they need,
Not what they want
Furthermore, all wars would stop
As well as the malice that it breeds
And all the ills that Man can conceive
With a wave of my hand
Would make them all realise
It's the life that you lead
Not the goods you can buy.

The Judas Kiss

They came on a cold February day
Seeking refuge in a place they called home
Fearing for their lives
Swapping the dangerous Indian heat
For the ice cold streets of Liverpool.

One man and his wife arriving
Trusting and believing: two innocent children
With a toddler and babe in arms
It was a case of live or die
Very simple – they choose life
Wouldn't you?

This was their country, wasn't it?
As doors slammed in their faces
The father, who fought for his land
Rewarded with a Judas kiss.

He was at Kohima, you know
Serving his grateful kingdom
Where he shot a Japanese soldier
Rifling through the dead man's pockets
Holding a photo of a family
Looking into the dead father's eyes
He saw himself.

A List for Pleasure

A warm summer's day
With a cooling breeze flowing by
In a colourful, fragrant garden
Myriad soporific sounds

Your partner's smiling face
The joy of a gurgling child
Splashing in the paddling pool

What a summer's day should be
A little heaven on earth.

A Memory

Under this grass, a dear one lies sleeping
My eyes are red with constantly weeping
Totally shocked and emotionally bleeding
Forever a piece of my heart will be grieving
A loved one is gone and my brain is unbelieving
All I can do is leave them in God's keeping.

The world has stopped: but people pass by
Busy with their lives, making me cry
I want to stop them and ask them why
They are not mourning my loved one who died.

December

December is my name
Spreading happiness my game
Dressed in my sexy red gown
Walking through the town
Luring the sad and surly
Into the frantic hurly burly
Together with my friends
Ensuring the spirit of Christmas extends

When the shopping is all complete
People putting up their feet
Whatever you believe
I remember that first Christmas Eve
Bringing to the forefront of the mind
Trying to remind all mankind
The hope and joy a baby brings
(It doesn't have to be a king!)
It's mother protects it from harm
As the child nestles in her arms

See the lady's face, her reason for being?
That's the miracle I'm seeing.

Dilemma

When a mad man rules the land
And people don't know where they stand
Where a cancerous evil slowly spreads
Seeping poison through everyone's heads
Every person living with the fear
Of the midnight knock upon their door
Huddled away: gone for evermore

You look at your child and fear
The future you thought was secure
Is not so secure as you thought
Silently you hatch a plan
To get save your children away from here
Fervently saying your prayers
If there's a God, please let them be spared
Somehow that miracle appears
Though you'll never see them again
At least you know they'll suffer no pain

But there's no miracle for you
You know what they will do
But your children will not hear
That midnight knock and fear
They have a chance to be free
In a land you hope will never see
How cruel some people can be.

First Meeting

I met him at my birthday party
It was last day of summer
How could I ever forget?
As he looked up
I saw his beautiful eyes
Like polished tigers-eye
Shining out from his face
Smiling at me
Taking my breath away

An unknown feeling, strange
A stranger, yet I knew him well
I knew that first meeting
Would last forever.

Flowerpower

I see myself as a flower
Thrusting my head skywards
To catch the bright sunlight
It warms and strengthens me
And makes my dreams take flight
When my flowers open
I startle all who see
For, while growing
Nobody noticed me.

For a Short Life

She touched my life
Like a sweet summer smile
Warming all of our days
Basking in the power she displayed

Kimberley's presence was barely a sigh
But she'll never be
Far from my mind
Nor her lovely ways

They say a good teacher
Is never ever forgotten
But it's not just the lessons
It's the bravery and strength
She portrayed

A sage lived in a child's eyes
Not an English rose,
But a clematis flower
Lifting her head to the sun

While we miss her so much
Her journey takes her on
But her song lingers on.

Tribute

The birds are not the same colour any more
But still soar high above those well loved shores
Guardians of all that was worth fighting for

The threat of invasion has long since gone
But dangerous days still lurk on and on
Our soldiers are still as brave and strong

But I remember hearing the singer of that song
When the country faced a dangerous, evil throng
She was the one who kept the spirit soaring on

Remembering still the words that she said
Showing that courage and compassion are not yet dead
Reminding us we have the legacy strength of those days

For the magic, simple melody and the singer
Yes, the singer of that song
Will be our country's symbol now and ever more
A simple message – but still worth fighting for.

Two Excited Children

It's Christmas Eve and so silent
You can hardly hear a heartbeat
Suddenly my two lovely children
Rushed in and started to speak

Their words tumbled excitedly over
Torrents shooting from their mouths
"The elves have been here again, Mum
They must have crept in tonight
We tried keep our eyes open
But their fairy dust made us sleep tight"

How much we looked forward to greeting them
Dressed in their magical clothes
We wanted to ask how Santa was feeling
Was Rudolph's navigation as hot as his nose?

We'd tell Santa what good children
That we've been for our Mum and Dad
Times are really hard now and they both look so sad
So we've behaved just like the angels
Who gave some shepherds a bad fright
Whilst announcing the good news currently
Breaking in Bethlehem that night

We can't wait for Christmas morning
When our empty stockings are filled
With chocolates and toys amongst the many
Other really good things

Mum and Dad are so happy
At least if only for one day
They tell us that God is a father
And his son was born today.

Armistice Day

The sky is heavy and grey
Joining the sombre mourning
Of this 90th Armistice Day
Always so cold and dank
As if the very air of the dead
Stands with us for the silence
Sparking memories of loss
Bringing the past to life

Not just the 'Glorious Dead'
Haunts my soul today
Living reminders of our wars
Fill our crowded streets
Unable to forget
The day the bullets started
and never ever ceased.

Bike

I step on a magic carpet
When I'm riding my bike
It's my ticket to freedom
For I used to walk for miles
Now that's all gone
I've received horrified looks
Devastating me
But when I'm sailing along
I'm just like anyone else
Just another rider
Such rapture!
No one is staring.

Last summer I rode
Along the Test Way
Pedalling along I felt
Like a goddess on her chariot
Or a Queen
Never thought I'd go
Along these leafy tracks
A memory locked forever
Stopping for an ice cream
Sweet Ambrosia!

Confidence via PD

I'm a woman of a certain age
Invisible
Lurking like a guilty conscience
In an unquiet mind
No one looks at me
Or sees the strength
Beneath the skin
I've learnt so much

From PD that is
Giving in return
Such confidence
Isn't that strange?
Looking the world in the eye
I have such power

Once I was afraid
Not now
Coping is my thing
I feel pretty again
My voice is stronger now
Believe me,
Making its presence known.

How often have I heard
(As the old saying goes)
'You don't know what you've got
Till it's gone'
My power comes from learning

To know what treasure you have
While it's still here.

Jacqui

She has a smile so wide
So warm, like summertime
But when you hear her voice
It's like the cool, bubbling water
You want on a hot, sultry day
That refreshes your body
Lightens the mood
And washes those blues away
A moment locked into your memory
Reprising
Whenever your throat is dry
Just thinking of that tinkling voice
You'll have no need of anything
The voice is all the refreshment you need.

Past

Have you ever heard that whisper?
Starting silently like a soft breeze
Getting louder as each year passes
It becomes a clarion call
So loud until you sit and listen
To the past and what it has to say.

I have felt like this for some time
Until that nagging sound made me move
Travelling to the national treasures of Kew
I felt so excited; and I knew
This is something I really had to do.

I got my great grandfather's record of service
Such a strange feeling, holding it close
It has a description of the man himself
But the pleasure of holding those bits of paper
From another time, just took my breath away.

We were strangers to each other
But I wouldn't exist with him.
So I've come to realise, that time travel is real
But it happens in your head, not a machine.

The strong voice is the engine
Your brain the pedal to take you there
The past is always with us
Just a minute away, just imagine it
And you've arrived.

Love Is Forever

Love is there forever
Whatever the day
The memory of first meeting
When our eyes locked
Is fixed in my mind
Never erased

Our lives have not been easy
And the years have flown
Perhaps only God knows where
But that's the way life goes
One thing I know
In another life I saw you
And in this one you are still here
Some things will never change.

Missy

You're pretty old now Missy
Being hatched in far off days
But you stand, a Queen in Waiting
Expecting people to listen to what you say

You are the oldest King Penguin at Birdland
The show is nothing without you
As you stand there looking so lovely
And cute as a penguin can be

Your coat may be bit tatty and walk with a limp
But you'll always be a star to me.

The Few

What was the weather like?
On that September day
Young men soaring above
The sky like Apollo
Their personal gift of light
Saviours from evil darkness
Silently encroaching
Trying to clutch our souls
Alone except for our hopes
Our prayers went with them

What were their thoughts?
Like naughty boys, flying
Having a laugh?
They were so young!
Newly ripened by the sun
Invincible, or so they thought
One brief round, a dive
A life now gone
The target not quite reached

What did those families do?
When that telegram arrived?
A woman bereft: grounded now
A bewildered child: parents stunned
Wreckage all around
A question we should ask,
If I may be so bold
Did we keep their dreams alive?

What were their names?
Biggles? Oh yes I know
How many brave unknown?
Their names engraved
At Runnymede
A potent document
Stands proud
Pointing to the sky.

The Sun

The sun is like a cat
With rays lightly stroking your back
The warmth puts a smile on your face
Making you love the human race
Your troubles vanish in an instant
You can't even see them in the distance
Winter cold is now gone
Spreading warmth to everyone
The feeling is like no other
The pleasure beyond measure.

Working

During my working life
I've never known such strife
When the computer system goes down
There's a universal wail all around.
We rely so much on machines
Too much, if you know what I mean!
We mustn't lose the human touch: the laugh, the smile
Which makes our lives mean so much.

To meet our workmates and exchange news
To discuss our thoughts and give our views
To show when we're happy or sad – or even hopping mad!
They help us feel happy, content and glad.

Jane's Message

I wish I knew you better
You're so rarely seen these days
A mere glimpse as you pass this way
And something I'm desperate to say
I have admired your optimism
Which you have in bounds
The strength which so strongly radiates
When you're around

A person so serene
That's what's special, you see
That's what I feel

I don't think I have even known
You have such abundant kindness
Which you're not slow to show
You've always a smile
How do you do it?
I don't know.

No wonder everyone who knows you
Loves you so much
A flower in the midst of the desert
And refreshing rain in June
You bring happiness to all you touch.

Do you remember the time we walked together
It was some months ago in lovely sunny weather
We were happily chatting

Then we went our separate ways
When I had walked on alone
I wish I had realised
I really wished I known you better.

The Knock

When I married my soldier
How love makes one forget!
When he marches off to war
My life seems to stop
There are people who fill my day
But when night time comes
All rational thought takes flight

During this silent world
When darkness reigns
Happy people sleep
But peace sadly eludes me
Lying all alone, pleading,
begging, listening, offering
silent prayers like a mantra
Please – don't send the knock
How I fear the knock!

That's my greatest fear
Every little sound
Is like an electric shock
The greatest fear of all
Is the Families' Officer's knock
Seeing the gates of Hades opening
Would make my heart stop.

They see my husband on TV
Does anyone think about me?
Sitting on my own
Watching the clock
Tick tock, tick tock, tick tock.

Reflections on the Lonely Walk

Hot sun, cool brain
What a soldier needs
In this terrain
As you begin
The lonely walk
Silently you start to talk
Of all the things you
have to look
So when you finally
reach the trap
You'll disengage
and go back

As you carefully
check the bomb
Someone is
looking in
Your fingers move
along and feel
You wonder who
is watching you
Hoping you
have got the thing
Not blowing all
to smithereens

You say the prayer
that they all say
"If it is my time
make it quick,
But, whatever please
don't let me
Bugger up.

When I'm here I feel alive
Every nerve, every vibe
But let me be lucky
and survive
To leave this harsh
and troubled place
Can't wait to hold
my loved ones tight
In a different time
and space.

Incorruptible

Time is money
But money cannot buy time
Whatever my father said
In a world where all is for sale
It is incorruptible
Unpredictable
When is our time?

Like a wave it rushes over
Bringing new life
Sweeping away the old
Silently it approaches
Then it recedes
But never returns
To the place where
The wave started to rise

All that is in the past
The wave moves again
And time moves in its
Silent waters.

Compass

I am small, insignificant
Unnoticed in your hand
But I have the power
To help you in unknown lands
I'm not so cuddly
As a teddy bear
But you'll always turn to me
When you're all alone
Unable to find home.

Sally Ann

She stood at the entrance to the shopping centre today
People walked by, with nothing much to say
Eyes averted, quickly scurried away
Thank you very much, but I'm too busy to stay

Was I the only one who saw her
Dressed in a well-known gown
Topped with an old fashioned Victorian hat
I would say she became invisible
If it wasn't for the frowns

Or is she standing for a truth no one to see
Does anyone want to acknowledge the good she can do?
I see her waiting like an angel in the dark
A silent statue: the conscience of this land
Helping the people who need a helping hand
A living symbol of the second chance

She's the Crisis at Christmas
The lone tender hand in the dark
Really like a modern Noah's Ark

Most of all she shows what she believes
A determined old lady
Who carries out the task she preaches
I wish you had stopped just to say hello
Please do so if she ever passes your way
Stop her and talk,
When you look into her eyes

They'll tell you the truth
Not some spin started by General Booth.

Mary Remembered

She's finally gone, that tiny woman
With a large heart. Ironic that, just
taking French leave, no fuss
for everyone. So like her!
Mrs Thatcher in her heyday
Couldn't match this Lady's
Iron will.

You taught me to cook rice
A good lesson: one cup of rice
Mixed with two and a half of water.
Perfection.

All the things I remember
Three women holding each other
Like rocks linked together
You were always the place of safety
And serenity shining through
Like a bright, welcoming light
I often wondered;
If your faith supported you
Or the other way around
You had compassion and
Love: you understood
Mostly.

Goodbye then, Mary
The last link to the past
From another privileged life

Saharanpore railways and tiffin
Memories of the British Raj
Lost forever.
But you will
Always be loved.

A Domestic Love Affair

You flick my switch said the kettle to the pot
I love the sexy colour of your skin
For red is the colour of the mood I'm in
My body is electrified whenever you come out
Everything inside me starts to heat to boiling point
Suddenly my passion mounts until I blow my top
But you don't see what an ardent lover you've got!

Signing Off

It's been lovely to hear your voice
Speaking hardly without breathing
Now I really have no choice
I can see husband slowly seething
Glancing at the clock
His eyes have done the talking
Woman for goodness sake
JUST STOP!

A Stolen Life

A young girl much misunderstood
In the days when they had to be good
Wanting to live so much more
Than a conventional woman's chore

Her family were so ashamed
Why couldn't she follow their game?
"It's not the way young ladies behave"
We will show her she must obey
The rules our society has made.

She's mad! So bad and dangerous!
Such conduct should not be discussed
What if this behaviour spreads?
Turning our own daughter's heads
Girls should marry their father's choice
Then submit their personalities and voice.

Lock her up! Take her away from our sight!
Society has a new sacrifice
We'll get rid of this blight
First her body, then her child, then her life.

This pretty girl, who had such a brilliant brain
Was driven totally insane!
Strapped down at night in her bed
In the morning, scrubbing floors instead.

You can't hear your guilt at all
And nobody is appalled
Like the silence from the padded cell
It changes not a thing: you are guilty as hell

Just tell me: who exactly is insane?
Why did nobody take the blame?

Swan Lake

The pair looked so graceful
Dancing on the water
Heads close together
Drooping like snowdrops
So shy welcoming in the spring

Fonteyn and Nureyev
But who would ever guess?
Starring in their best production
Sliding across the lake
In their sparkling white gowns.

The Tower

The sun has set in London
On this chilly, January night
The show closed for the day
The tourists head for home
As night wears on in the city

The Tower sits like an empress
Wearing her royal gown
Clothed in a swathes of light
Such a powerful sight!
If only those walls could talk!
How many ghosts still walk?

I'll swear those walls seep names
Of innocence betrayed.
Lady Jane grey
Manipulated and blamed
For her parents plotting ways
Dragged on to Tower Hill
Her last five minutes of fame
Until the curtain falls

But, not today
I hear the walls say
We don't use Traitors Gate
In this modern age.

But, all the same…

Dangerous Steps

Come into my parlour said the spider to the fly
My fine hospitality is well known far and wide
I'll look after you – do not be surprised!
I will take good care of you, and you will thrive
So the innocent fly took a step inside
Dear reader, we know how this tragic story ends
But the fly thought he'd found a kind and loving friend
So, when you look into those dark, hypnotic eyes
Remember that a hungry spider always, always lies.

Hostage

Help! I'm being held hostage
And my body will not say
Exactly how much I have to pay
In fact it tells me nothing
It has declared UDI
Doing it's own thing
Stopping on a whim
Not even the police
Can establish my release.

What Makes You What You Are?

This is my journey
Mine and mine alone
I've had great success
I've had great sadness
Followed by my feeling
That joy will always be mine
If I can only see it

Yours is an interesting question
The answer is anyone's guess
All I will offer is my mother's bequest
The strength she has is endless
She'll never ever quit
A survivor
(we'll forget the short, rotund body
Which she has kindly donated to me)

We are like each other, my mother and I
What defines me mostly is I'm human
I love, I live, I learn then I take my leave
Watching the children take this
Mad roller-coaster ride!

Shoes

I am baby's first shoes
Tiny, warm, pink and
a strong internal support;
To help my little owner
Make her first tiny steps
To fulfil her destiny
It won't be long
Before I too sit like she does
She will grow and no longer need me
Then I shall sit on the shelf and
Watch her grow; with a job well done
Feeling proud because it was
Me who gave her the confidence
To stand tall and proud
As she takes on the world.

Teenager

You're a woman with a child's eyes
And your hormones are driving you wild
But will you promise? Oh please try
To show more Dr Jekyll and less Mr Hyde?

For Kitty on Her Birthday

You used to sit quietly for hours
Toys scattered on the floor
Not any more
The pretty baby turned toddler
Has metamorphosed into a beautiful girl

Tomorrow you are thirteen
Childhood slipping away
Turning towards tomorrow
As you walk along your way
A way I think you've chosen
A long time ago

How can one so young
Be so intelligent?
And determined
But that's you
As lovely inside as outside
Be assured we love you.

Pops

Pops said goodbye to me today
He said he had to catch a train
From his hospital bed
I told him he wasn't going anywhere

He'd lived so many years
Seen many things
Some not pleasant
But he could still smile

He told such stories
When a person dies
so do their memories
A precious book on former days
slams shut – Access denied!

But he had such a vibrant spirit
So much kindness
So much love
Such faith.

One dark cold January night
we were summoned
Slowly and silently
Pops finally caught his train alone
But how I bitterly regret
Not saying that final goodbye.

The Invisible Woman

I'm sitting with some friends
After having a lovely meal
Listening to the chatter
But every time I try to speak
I'm ignored so I say
"Knock knock, I'm here
Hello can you see me
I'm over here"
I thought I was large
Enough to be seen
But maybe I'm in a dream

I know it's not easy to speak
My voice sometimes goes to a squeak
That doesn't mean I have nothing to say
So please don't talk over me I pray
I know I have Parkinson's Disease
But there's one thing you should
Know about me
I know it's hard to believe
But I'm human too
Just like you.

Johnnie Walker

This Christmas I've woken up
To a very pleasant surprise
Johnnie Walker
The man my husband describes
As the man with the laughter
In his voice: bubbling over
You can almost see it shining
From his eyes

I saw him when he came to The Lights
I was keen to see hear his memories
Of Radio Caroline
A much beloved pirate ship
They gave our generation a voice
And a sound all of their own
A time of exploration, a new dawn rising

Those days were very special
We were going to change the world!
But, to a certain extent
The world changed us
I have always said
It's the journey, not the destination
Which counts – and that is truer for you

Thank you, Johnnie, for your company
I hope it lasts for many years longer
This you will not like, but it must be said I'm afraid
You are like Terry Wogan, you understand you see

No judgement, just compassion
Empathatic too
You are a friend indeed.

Memories of Jane

You have left a mark on each one of our lives
A remarkable woman: taken long before your time
But the memory of you will never ever die
I will always see the sweet, intelligent face
Which crinkled with laughter and lived at a spanking pace
You touched everybody and gave life all you'd got
Even though the winter has shown its icy frown
How can anyone ever let it get them down?
For I know the spring will return and the sun will shine
Giving life to the garden everywhere it goes
In the morning sun – and as everybody knows
A sturdy flower defies the cold, uncaring snow
The memory of you will bloom everywhere it grows
I will see your face in that perfect English rose.

Home Thoughts from Afghanistan

Oh to be in England at any time of year
Even on a rainy day, it's better than being here
England is where my heart lies
Within my family's mind and eyes
I can see them waiting now
Wishing the time would fly
So I will come home
No matter how

When I look out at these dusty streets
Full of strangers, blood and death
 I dream about those green hills
And the hazy days by the sea
That's where I want to be
With the people I love

I want to come home
Desperately
Alive, and free.

If Only

Life is a dream
Which soon fades away
It passes like lightning
Sometimes leaving a mark
Mostly it seems we never say
Exactly what we meant to say
The four saddest words
In the whole wide world
Are "I wish I had"
Before life drifted away.

Make your life count
Live your dream
Don't let the days
Just fade away
If you're lucky
You'll find your love

Don't let a day pass
Without letting them know
You love them very much
So when it's time for you to go
As you silently slip away
Your last words won't be
"Oh, if only…"

Lightning Source UK Ltd.
Milton Keynes UK
05 April 2011

170389UK00001B/116/P